AF454176

FROM DATA TO DECISIONS:

Driving Performance in the Age of Analytics

Babatunde Yusuf

ISBN: 978-4-0240-6374-6

Publishing by:
Emphaloz Publishing House
Abuja, Nigeria.
www.emphaloz.com
publish@emphaloz.com

Cover Design by Emphaloz Digital

A catalogue record of this book will be available from the National Library of Nigeria.

PREFACE

In an age where information is abundant and technology evolves at an unprecedented pace, the ability to harness data stands as a crucial determinant of success across all sectors. "From Data to Decisions: Driving Performance in the Age of Analytics" is crafted to demystify the complexities of data analytics and equip you with the knowledge and tools necessary to transform data into actionable insights.

This book is not merely a collection of methodologies; it is a guide to thinking analytically, fostering a data-centric mindset that can discern and leverage opportunities hidden within vast datasets. Each chapter is designed to build upon the last, creating a comprehensive framework that progresses from foundational concepts to sophisticated techniques and strategic applications in various industries.

This book endeavors to bridge the gap between traditional decision-making processes and modern data-driven techniques through a blend of theoretical insights, practical advice, and real-world case studies. It aims to empower professionals, business leaders, and aspiring data scientists alike to make informed, data-backed decisions that drive performance, innovation, and growth.

As you embark on this journey, remember that the data analytics landscape is continually evolving. The principles and practices discussed herein serve not only as a roadmap for current methodologies but also as a springboard into the future developments that will shape the next era of analytics.

Table of Contents

INTRODUCTION

In today's digitally-driven world, the ability to make decisions backed by concrete data is not just an advantage; it is a necessity. "From Data to Decisions: Driving Performance in the Age of Analytics" serves as a pivotal guide for individuals seeking to understand and apply data analytics to enhance decision-making processes.

The journey through data analytics begins with the foundational elements: understanding the nature and significance of data. From small businesses to multinational corporations, the reliance on data transcends industries, reshaping strategies and outcomes in profound ways. This book breaks down complex analytical concepts into understandable segments, ensuring readers from all professional backgrounds can grasp and apply these insights effectively.

Each chapter of the book progressively builds on knowledge and skills, introducing readers to a wide range of analytical techniques. From the basics of collecting and managing data to the more intricate tasks of predictive and prescriptive analytics, this guide covers the entire spectrum. Our aim is not just to inform but to transform the reader's approach to data, equipping them with the tools to ask the right questions and craft strategies that lead to actionable insights.

Moreover, this book addresses the challenges and ethical considerations that come with data analytics. In an era where data breaches and privacy concerns are rampant, understanding how to navigate these issues responsibly is crucial. We provide a balanced view, discussing the potential pitfalls and ethical dilemmas that data scientists and organizations may encounter.

As you delve into the pages of this book, you will find a blend of theoretical frameworks, practical applications, and real-world case studies. These elements are designed to not only illustrate the power of data analytics but also to inspire innovative approaches to problem-solving and decision-making.

By the end of this book, you will have gained a comprehensive understanding of how data can be transformed into valuable insights that drive strategic decisions. Whether you are a seasoned professional seeking to refine your analytical skills or a newcomer eager to make your mark in the world of data, "From Data to

Decisions" is your essential guide to navigating the complex landscape of data analytics.

CHAPTER 1
The Evolution of Decision-Making

In the ever-changing landscape of business and technology, the ability to make informed decisions based on robust data analysis has become paramount. This shift from intuition-based to data-driven decision-making marks a significant evolution in how organizations operate. In the past, executives often relied on experience and gut feeling to guide their choices. Today, data analytics offers a more objective foundation for these decisions, providing insights that can significantly enhance accuracy and outcomes.

The transition to data-driven practices didn't happen overnight. It has been facilitated by advances in technology, increases in computing power, and the exponential growth of data generation. These changes have allowed businesses of all sizes to implement sophisticated analytics techniques that were once the preserve of large corporations with vast resources.

Historical Context

Historically, data has always played a role in decision-making, but its use was often limited by technology and expertise. In the early 20th century, simple statistical methods and manual data collection sufficed. However, as the century progressed, the advent of computers and the development of more complex statistical methods expanded the possibilities of what could be achieved with data. The real transformation began with the digital revolution. With more data available than ever before, the challenge shifted from data collection to data management and interpretation. The introduction of relational databases in the 1970s and the subsequent development of the internet in the 1990s democratized data access and analysis, setting the stage for the advanced data analytics we use today.

The concept of Big Data emerged as a pivotal turning point in the history of analytics. It refers to the vast volumes of data that are collected, processed, and analyzed to support decision-making. Big Data is characterized by its volume, velocity, and variety, and handling it requires advanced tools and technologies, such as machine learning algorithms and cloud computing. The impact of Big Data is profound. It allows organizations to perform market analysis, predict customer behavior, optimize operations, and much more, all in real-time. The insights gleaned from Big Data analytics can lead to more effective marketing strategies, improved customer service, and increased operational efficiency.

Theoretical Foundations

The backbone of data-driven decision-making lies in its theoretical foundations—statistics, probability, and computer science. Understanding these concepts is crucial for anyone looking to master data analytics. Statistics provide the tools to make sense of the data, probability theory helps to assess the likelihood of future events, and computer science offers the algorithms and computational techniques necessary to process large datasets. These theories are not static; they evolve as new challenges and technologies emerge. The ongoing development of these foundations ensures that data analytics remains a dynamic and growing field, continually enhancing its capability to support decision-making.

Consider the case of a global retail chain that implemented data analytics to refine its inventory management. By analyzing sales data, customer preferences, and supply chain logistics, the company could predict which products would be in high demand and adjust their stock levels accordingly. This not only reduced inventory costs but also improved customer satisfaction by ensuring popular items were always available.

Integrating Data into Decision-Making

Integrating data into the decision-making process can be challenging. It requires not only the right tools and technologies but also a cultural shift within the organization. Employees at all levels must understand the importance of data and be trained to interpret and use it effectively. Organizations often start this integration by identifying key decision points where data can have the most significant impact. From there, they develop metrics and analytics to guide these decisions, gradually expanding the use of data as comfort and familiarity with the processes grow.

Ethical Considerations

As the reliance on data increases, so do the ethical considerations. Data-driven decisions must be made responsibly, with an awareness of potential biases in data collection and analysis. Organizations must ensure that their data practices do not inadvertently discriminate against any group or individual. Furthermore, privacy concerns are paramount. With increasing regulations like the GDPR in Europe and the CCPA in California, companies must be vigilant about how they collect, store, and use data to avoid legal and reputational risks.

As we look to the future, the role of data in decision-making will only grow. The next frontier includes advances in artificial intelligence and machine learning, which promise to unlock even more sophisticated insights from data. However, the human element will remain crucial; technology is a tool, but the ultimate decisions must still be made by people. The evolution of decision-making from intuition to data-driven is a testament to the advancements in technology and analytics. By understanding the historical context, theoretical foundations, and practical applications, organizations can harness the power of data to make informed decisions that drive performance and innovation.

CHAPTER 2
Fundamentals of Data Analysis

In today's data-centric environment, mastering the basics of data analysis is crucial for anyone aiming to harness its capabilities for informed decision-making. This chapter delivers a comprehensive introduction to the fundamental concepts, techniques, and methodologies integral to proficient data analysis. By exploring these foundational elements, readers will gain the necessary skills to effectively interpret and utilize data, thereby enhancing their strategic decision-making processes.

Understanding Data Types and Structures

Data analysis begins with a clear understanding of the types of data you will encounter and the structures that can organize this data efficiently. Essentially, data can be categorized into quantitative (numerical) and qualitative (categorical) types. Each type requires different analysis techniques and tools. For instance, numerical data might be analyzed through statistical means, while categorical data could be better understood through classification or segmentation techniques. Moreover, the way data is structured plays a crucial role in analysis. Structured data is organized into databases with clear definitions of what each field represents, such as SQL databases. Unstructured data, such as emails, video, or social media posts, is more amorphous and often requires more sophisticated techniques, such as natural language processing or image recognition, to decipher and utilize effectively.

Key Principles of Data Collection

Effective data analysis relies heavily on the quality of data collected. Therefore, understanding how to gather quality data is fundamental. The first principle of data collection is defining clear objectives: knowing what you need from the data helps in designing a collection process that can achieve your goals effectively. It's also crucial to ensure that data collection methods are ethical and respect privacy concerns, adhering to regulations and laws applicable in the relevant jurisdictions. Sampling is another critical aspect of data collection. Whether using random sampling or stratified approaches, the goal is to ensure that the sample accurately represents the larger population. This avoids biases that could skew the analysis and lead to erroneous conclusions.

Once the data is collected, the next step is to apply statistical methods to derive insights. Descriptive statistics summarize data points and are crucial for providing a clear picture of what the data looks like. Measures such as mean, median, mode, and standard deviation are among the most commonly used. For deeper insights, inferential statistics are employed to make predictions or inferences about a population based on a sample of data. Techniques such as regression analysis, hypothesis testing, and variance analysis are powerful tools for understanding relationships between variables and making predictions about future trends.

Visualization is a pivotal part of data analysis, transforming complex results into understandable and actionable visual representations. Tools and techniques like line graphs, bar charts, heat maps, and scatter plots help stakeholders quickly understand trends, patterns, and outliers in the data. Effective visualization requires an understanding of both the data and the audience, ensuring that the visuals are not only accurate but also accessible to those who need to interpret them.

To implement data analysis effectively, one must navigate the integration of these techniques into the daily operations of an organization. This often starts with the adoption of appropriate technologies and platforms that can handle the volume, velocity, and variety of data typical in today's business environments. Tools like R for statistical computing and analysis, Python with powerful libraries like Pandas and NumPy, and BI tools like Tableau for visualization, are indispensable in the toolkit of a data analyst.

Moreover, fostering a culture that values data-driven decision-making is essential. This involves training teams, setting up processes for continuous data evaluation and feedback, and creating a mindset where decisions are regularly backed by data insights.

Ethical Considerations in Data Analysis

As data analysis becomes more integral to organizational strategies, ethical considerations must be at the forefront. Ensuring data accuracy, respecting user privacy, and maintaining transparency about how data is used are all crucial to ethical data analysis. Furthermore, analysts must be vigilant against biases that can be inherent in data or introduced during the analysis process. Regular audits and checks, diverse teams, and adherence to ethical guidelines are best practices that help mitigate these issues.

Mastering the fundamentals of data analysis opens up a world of possibilities for enhancing decision-making capabilities. By understanding the types of data, principles of collection, statistical methods, and effective visualization techniques, businesses and individuals can unlock valuable insights from their data. As this chapter closes, we are reminded that the journey of data analysis is one of continuous learning and adaptation. With a solid foundation in these fundamentals, you are well-equipped to explore more complex techniques and applications detailed in the subsequent chapters.

CHAPTER 3
Data Collection and Management

In the field of data analytics, the saying "Garbage in, garbage out" holds significant weight, as the quality of insights is profoundly dependent on the quality of the data collected and managed. This chapter thoroughly explores the crucial strategies for effective data collection and management, which are vital steps for any data-driven initiative. It highlights the importance of establishing robust data governance frameworks that define who can access and control data, ensuring data integrity and security. Furthermore, the chapter discusses the need for implementing comprehensive data validation and cleaning processes to remove inaccuracies and inconsistencies, which can drastically skew analytics results.

We also examine techniques for data integration, which involve consolidating data from diverse sources to provide a holistic view of the information, enhancing the accuracy of the insights generated. Additionally, the chapter covers the use of advanced technologies like machine learning algorithms for predictive cleaning, which can anticipate and correct errors in data collection in real time. Another critical aspect discussed is the continuous monitoring and updating of data to keep it relevant as business environments evolve. This not only helps in maintaining the accuracy of the data set but also ensures that the data-driven strategies remain aligned with current business objectives. By emphasizing these strategies, this chapter aims to guide organizations on how to cultivate high-quality datasets that are instrumental in driving reliable and actionable analytics outcomes.

Data Collection Fundamentals

The process of data collection begins with a clear identification of objectives. What decisions need to be supported by the data? What specific insights are sought? Answering these questions helps in designing a data collection strategy that is not only targeted but also efficient. As Albert Einstein famously said, "Not everything that can be counted counts, and not everything that counts can be counted." This highlights the importance of focusing on relevant data points that directly support business objectives. Once the goals are set, the next step is choosing the right data collection methods. These methods range from automated data capture in a digital environment to manual data entry in more traditional settings. Each method has its own set of challenges and advantages, and the choice largely depends on the context in which the data is being gathered. For digital data, tools, and software that track user interactions provide a wealth of information, whereas surveys and interviews can be better for gathering qualitative insights.

Data Quality and Integrity

Ensuring data quality is paramount. Poor data quality can lead to misleading analyses and potentially costly business decisions. Data cleansing practices should be implemented to check for the accuracy, completeness, and reliability of the data. Techniques such as data validation and cleaning help in correcting errors and filling missing values, ensuring the integrity of datasets for analysis. Data integrity is equally crucial. It refers to maintaining and assuring the accuracy and consistency of data over its entire lifecycle. Effective data management strategies must include robust data governance policies that address data integrity. This includes setting standards and procedures for data usage and handling to avoid common pitfalls such as data redundancy and fragmentation.

Data Management Techniques

Effective data management is a dynamic and continuous process. It involves organizing, storing, and maintaining the data collected in a manner that makes it easily accessible and usable. Technologies such as databases and data warehousing are fundamental to efficient data management. They provide structured ways to store large volumes of data, making it easier to retrieve and analyze when needed. However, as the volume of data grows exponentially, traditional data management techniques can become cumbersome and inefficient. Here, advanced solutions like cloud storage and big data platforms come into play. They offer scalable and flexible options for managing large datasets, with the added advantages of enhanced security and accessibility. As the saying goes, "The world is one big data problem," and modern data management technologies are crucial in solving this problem by ensuring that data is not just stored but is also meaningful and accessible.

In today's digital age, data security and privacy are more important than ever. With data breaches and cyber-attacks becoming more frequent, protecting sensitive data is a top priority for any organization. Implementing strong security measures such as encryption, access controls, and regular security audits can help safeguard data from unauthorized access and breaches. Privacy is another critical aspect of data management. Organizations must ensure they comply with data protection regulations such as GDPR in Europe and CCPA in California. These regulations enforce strict guidelines on how personal data should be collected, stored, and used, ensuring that individuals' privacy rights are respected.

Integration with Analytics

Once data is collected and managed properly, integrating it into analytical tools and platforms is the next step. This integration allows businesses to extract actionable insights from their data, facilitating informed decision-making. Tools such as SQL for data manipulation, Python for data analysis, and business intelligence platforms like Tableau for data visualization are integral to this process. Integrating data into analytics should be seamless and efficient, enabling organizations to respond quickly to market changes and internal dynamics. It's about turning data into a strategic asset that can provide a competitive advantage in the marketplace.

Managing data effectively is a fundamental aspect of any successful data analytics initiative. As we have explored in this chapter, collecting high-quality data, maintaining its integrity, ensuring its security and privacy, and integrating it effectively into analytical tools are all crucial steps. These practices are not merely technical necessities but strategic endeavors that require thoughtful planning and execution. Remember, as W. Edwards Deming once stated, "In God we trust, all others must bring data." This encapsulates the essence of our modern data-driven world, where reliable data is the cornerstone of trust and the catalyst for insightful decision-making.

CHAPTER 4
Tools and Technologies for Analytics

In the fast-changing world of data analytics, the tools and technologies utilized play a crucial role in enhancing the efficiency and effectiveness of the insights garnered. This chapter provides an in-depth exploration of the contemporary tools and technologies that are essential for anyone engaged in data analysis, focusing on their applications, benefits, and the considerations necessary for successful integration. We discuss a range of tools from advanced data management platforms, such as Hadoop and Apache Spark, which facilitate the processing of large datasets, to sophisticated analytics software like SAS, R, and Python that offer powerful statistical and predictive capabilities. Additionally, we explore visualization tools like Tableau and Power BI that enable analysts to convert complex data into understandable and actionable visual representations.

The chapter also covers emerging technologies like artificial intelligence and machine learning algorithms that are redefining predictive analytics by automating data analysis and decision-making processes. Furthermore, we address the importance of integrating these tools into existing business systems seamlessly, considering factors like scalability, security, and cost-efficiency. By doing so, organizations can ensure that their data analytics practices are not only advanced in terms of technology but also aligned with their strategic objectives, thereby maximizing the return on investment in data analytics technologies. This comprehensive overview aims to equip data professionals with the knowledge to choose and implement the right tools that will significantly amplify their analytic capabilities and drive better business outcomes.

The Breadth of Analytical Tools

Data analytics tools range from simple descriptive statistics software to advanced predictive and prescriptive analytics platforms. Each tool serves a specific purpose and is chosen based on the complexity of the task and the data involved. For straightforward tasks, tools like Microsoft Excel or Google Sheets might suffice with their built-in functions for statistical analysis and data visualization. However, as the complexity and volume of data increase, more robust solutions become necessary.

For more in-depth statistical analysis, software like R and Python, with its extensive libraries including Pandas, NumPy, and SciPy, are indispensable. R is particularly favored in academic and research settings for its wide range of packages and its ability to handle complex statistical computations. Python, on the other hand, is renowned for its simplicity and flexibility, making it a popular choice among data scientists for data manipulation, cleaning, and analysis. Both R and Python are supported by vibrant communities that contribute to a constantly evolving array of libraries and tools, ensuring that they remain at the forefront of analytics technologies. This community-driven development model means that they can quickly adapt to new analytical methodologies as they emerge.

Data Visualization Tools

When it comes to data visualization, tools like Tableau, Power BI, and QlikView offer powerful functionalities to transform complex data sets into intuitive and insightful visual representations. Tableau is particularly noted for its user-friendly interface and the ability to create interactive dashboards that can be understood by professionals at all levels within an organization. Power BI, provided by Microsoft, integrates seamlessly with other Microsoft products and offers robust data connectivity and visualization capabilities. These tools not only help in visualizing static data but also enable users to explore data dynamically, manipulate views, and drill down into specifics, providing a more granular understanding of the underlying data. The interactive capabilities of these tools allow decision-makers to explore scenarios and outcomes effectively, enhancing their ability to make informed decisions based on real-time data insights.

Big Data Technologies

For handling large volumes of data, technologies such as Hadoop and Spark are critical. Apache Hadoop is an open-source framework that allows for the distributed processing of large data sets across clusters of computers using simple programming models. It is designed to scale up from a single server to thousands of machines, each offering local computation and storage. Similarly, Apache Spark is known for its speed and ease of use in handling big datasets. Spark's in-memory cluster computing increases the processing speed of an application and is particularly useful for data algorithms that require iterative access to data. These big data technologies are complemented by database management systems like MySQL, MongoDB, and Cassandra, which provide the infrastructure for storing and managing large datasets. The choice between these systems often depends on the specific needs of the project, such as the speed of data retrieval required and the nature of the data being stored.

Cloud-Based Analytics

The rise of cloud computing has transformed data analytics by providing scalable resources on demand. Cloud platforms such as AWS, Google Cloud, and Azure offer services that allow businesses to store and analyze massive amounts of data without the need for significant upfront investment in physical infrastructure. These platforms provide tools that cover the entire analytics process, from data ingestion and storage to analysis and visualization, all hosted on the cloud. The benefits of cloud-based analytics include not only scalability and cost-efficiency but also enhanced collaboration. Teams can access the same data and tools from anywhere, making it easier to work together on analytical projects. The cloud also offers advanced security features that help protect sensitive data, which is particularly important in industries like finance and healthcare where data privacy is critical.

Integrating Analytics Tools into Business Processes

Integrating these tools and technologies into business processes requires careful planning and consideration. It involves not only technical implementation but also aligning with the organization's data strategy and training the workforce to use these tools effectively. The integration process often starts with a pilot project, which helps in understanding the practical challenges and benefits before a full-scale rollout. Successful integration also depends on having a clear data governance framework in place. This framework should address data quality, security, and privacy concerns and ensure that the data analytics efforts are in line with the business objectives and compliant with relevant regulations.

As we wrap up this exploration of the tools and technologies essential for data analytics, it's clear that the choice of tools can have a profound impact on the insights derived. Whether it's through enhancing data visualization capabilities, speeding up data processing, or providing flexible, scalable solutions via the cloud, these technologies empower organizations to harness the full potential of their data.

In the chapters that follow, we will continue to build on this foundation, exploring how these tools can be applied to specific analytical challenges and decision-making processes. Remember, as data continues to grow in volume and importance, staying updated with these technologies will be key to maintaining a competitive edge in the data-driven world.

CHAPTER 5
Mastering Descriptive Analytics

Descriptive analytics serves as the foundational pillar of data-driven decision-making, offering critical insights into past performance by meticulously analyzing historical data. This chapter delves deep into the concepts, techniques, and tools associated with descriptive analytics, emphasizing their vital role in extracting meaningful patterns and trends that inform strategic business decisions. We explore a variety of statistical methods that are central to descriptive analytics, including measures of central tendency (mean, median, mode), measures of variability (range, variance, standard deviation), and correlation coefficients. These techniques help organizations understand variations in their data, identify relationships between variables, and summarize vast datasets into actionable insights.

Additionally, the chapter highlights the array of tools used to implement descriptive analytics, from basic spreadsheet applications to more sophisticated data visualization software and BI platforms. These tools enable businesses to present their data visually through charts, graphs, and dashboards, making it easier to communicate findings across the organization.

We also examine real-world applications of descriptive analytics across different industries, showcasing how businesses utilize these insights to benchmark their performance, monitor operational efficiency, and guide budget planning and resource allocation. Through detailed examples, the chapter illustrates how descriptive analytics not only aids in understanding what has happened in the past but also sets the stage for more advanced forms of analytics, such as predictive and prescriptive analytics, thereby creating a comprehensive framework for strategic decision-making.

The Essence of Descriptive Analytics

Descriptive analytics involves summarizing vast amounts of data to make it understandable and actionable. This domain of analytics focuses on answering the question, "What has happened?" by utilizing historical data. Through methods such as statistical analysis, data aggregation, and data visualization, descriptive analytics helps businesses understand their operations, market conditions, and customer behaviors in profound detail. The process starts with data aggregation; the data collected from various sources is cleaned and compiled into a digestible format. Statistical techniques are then applied to measure trends, variability, and average performance. For instance, a retailer might use descriptive analytics to understand seasonal fluctuations in sales or to benchmark performance against past years.

Techniques and Tools for Descriptive Analytics

Several key techniques are pivotal in descriptive analytics. These include:

1. **Statistical Measures**: These are fundamental and include measures of central tendency (mean, median, mode) and measures of variability (range, variance, standard deviation). These statistics provide a snapshot of data distributions and are critical for accurate data interpretation.

2. **Data Visualization**: Tools like histograms, pie charts, bar charts, and line graphs translate statistical measures into visual formats that are easier to comprehend and share. Advanced tools such as Tableau, Microsoft Power BI, and Qlik Sense enhance this capability by allowing interactive data exploration, which can highlight trends and outliers more effectively.

3. **Correlation Analysis**: This technique assesses the relationship between variables, helping organizations to identify factors that influence their outcomes significantly. For example, a supermarket chain might use correlation analysis to find out which products are frequently bought together.

The choice of tools for descriptive analytics can vary depending on the specific needs and technical environment of the organization. However, software solutions like SAS, SPSS, and Excel remain popular for their robust statistical capabilities and user-friendly interfaces.

Applying Descriptive Analytics to Business Scenarios

The application of descriptive analytics extends across various domains of business:

- **Sales and Marketing**: Businesses use descriptive analytics to track and improve campaign performance, customer engagement, and overall sales effectiveness. By analyzing past sales data, companies can identify successful products, optimal pricing strategies, and effective marketing channels.

- **Supply Chain Management**: Descriptive analytics helps in monitoring inventory levels, supplier performance, and logistics operations. This analysis ensures that supply chain inefficiencies are identified and addressed promptly.

- **Financial Management**: In finance, descriptive analytics is used to manage cash flow, control costs, and assess financial performance against budgets and forecasts. Analyzing historical financial data helps in identifying trends that are crucial for future financial planning.

- **Customer Service**: By analyzing data from past interactions with customers, businesses can identify common issues, track the resolution time, and improve service delivery. This not only enhances customer satisfaction but also optimizes resource allocation in customer service departments.

Integrating Descriptive Analytics into Decision-Making

To effectively integrate descriptive analytics into business decision-making, organizations must ensure that data flows seamlessly across various departments and that the insights are accessible to all decision-makers. This integration often involves setting up centralized data repositories and employing business intelligence platforms that provide real-time access to descriptive analytics.

Moreover, fostering a data-driven culture is essential. This means training employees to understand and utilize data analytics in their daily decision-making processes. When the workforce is comfortable with data interpretation and application, the organization can fully leverage the insights generated by descriptive analytics.

Challenges and Considerations

Despite its immense value, implementing descriptive analytics is not without challenges. Data quality is a significant concern; inaccurate or incomplete data can lead to wrong conclusions. Additionally, integrating data from disparate sources into a coherent analytics framework often requires substantial time and resources.

Furthermore, there's a risk of becoming overly reliant on historical data. While descriptive analytics provides valuable insights, it is inherently backward-looking and does not account for future uncertainties. Organizations must complement these insights with predictive and prescriptive analytics to build a more comprehensive analytics strategy.

Descriptive analytics is a critical component of business analytics, offering detailed insights into past performance and operational effectiveness. By understanding the techniques and tools of descriptive analytics, and by applying these insights strategically, businesses can enhance their decision-making processes, improve operational efficiencies, and better respond to customer needs. As organizations continue to navigate through vast amounts of data, the role of descriptive analytics will remain fundamental in translating complex datasets into actionable business intelligence. In the subsequent chapters, we will explore how to build on these insights with predictive analytics, further enhancing the capability to not just understand the past but also to predict the future.

CHAPTER 6
Exploring Predictive Analytics

Predictive analytics marks a substantial advancement from descriptive analytics, offering insights not merely into past occurrences but also projecting future possibilities. This chapter examines the methodologies, tools, and real-world applications of predictive analytics, illustrating how it enables organizations to anticipate events and make proactive decisions. We explore various statistical techniques and machine learning algorithms that are foundational to predictive analytics, such as regression analysis, time series forecasting, and pattern recognition. These methodologies help in identifying trends, predicting customer behavior, and forecasting market changes.

The chapter also highlights a range of tools from simple statistical software to complex analytics platforms that facilitate the implementation of predictive models. By integrating these tools, businesses can harness large volumes of data to generate accurate forecasts that inform strategic planning.

Furthermore, we delve into diverse sectors such as finance, healthcare, retail, and manufacturing to demonstrate how predictive analytics is applied in practice. In finance, it predicts stock market trends and credit risks; in healthcare, it forecasts patient outcomes and disease spread; in retail, it anticipates consumer purchasing behaviors; and in manufacturing, it predicts equipment failures and maintenance needs. Through these applications, the chapter shows how predictive analytics not only anticipates the future but also empowers organizations to act upon these insights, enhancing efficiency and gaining a competitive advantage.

Understanding Prescriptive Analytics

Predictive analytics uses statistical techniques and machine learning models to analyze current and historical data to make predictions about future events. These predictions are made through models that identify patterns and trends within large data sets. As Richard Branson famously stated, "You don't learn to walk by following rules. You learn by doing, and by falling over," and similarly, predictive models iteratively improve as they "learn" from the data processed. The core of predictive analytics lies in its ability to provide actionable insights based on data, enabling businesses to mitigate risks, seize opportunities, and streamline operations. For instance, in the finance sector, predictive analytics is used to assess loan risks by predicting the likelihood of a borrower defaulting on a loan.

Techniques Used in Predictive Analytics

The techniques used in predictive analytics vary widely but typically include the following:

- **Regression Analysis**: This is used to understand relationships between variables and predict a continuous outcome. For example, a retailer might use regression to predict sales volumes based on historical sales data and other variables like marketing spend and seasonal factors.

- **Classification Models**: These are used to categorize data into labels. For instance, email spam filters use classification models to determine whether an email is spam or not based on its content and sender.

- **Time Series Forecasting**: This involves making predictions about future events based on known past events. It is widely used in stock market predictions, weather forecasting, and demand forecasting in retail.

- **Machine Learning Algorithms**: Techniques such as decision trees, random forests, and neural networks are used to make more complex predictions that can adapt over time as more data becomes available.

Implementing Predictive Analytics in Various Industries

Predictive analytics has proven its versatility and effectiveness across a wide range of industries, showcasing its capacity to transform data into actionable insights. This powerful tool leverages historical data and algorithms to forecast future trends and behaviors, enabling businesses to make well-informed decisions. Its applications span from healthcare, where it predicts patient outcomes, to retail, optimizing inventory management. Furthermore, it enhances financial services by assessing credit risk and detecting fraudulent activities, thereby illustrating its broad applicability and transformative potential in various sectors, including:

- **Healthcare**: Hospitals use predictive analytics to forecast patient admissions and manage staff allocations efficiently. Predictive models can also identify patients at high risk of chronic diseases, allowing for early intervention.

- **Retail**: Retailers use predictive analytics to manage inventory and create personalized marketing strategies that target customers based on their buying habits and preferences.

- **Banking and Finance**: Financial institutions use predictive analytics for credit scoring, risk management, and fraud detection, significantly reducing losses due to bad loans or fraudulent transactions.

- **Manufacturing**: In manufacturing, predictive maintenance techniques predict equipment failures before they occur, reducing downtime and maintenance costs.

Challenges in Predictive Analytics

While predictive analytics can provide significant benefits, it also comes with its own set of challenges. Data quality remains a crucial issue; predictive models are only as good as the data fed into them. Moreover, developing predictive models requires a deep understanding of both the techniques used and the domains to which they are applied, necessitating a significant investment in skilled personnel. Another challenge is the interpretation of model outputs. Predictive models can be complex, and their workings are not easily understandable to non-experts, which can lead to resistance to adopting predictive insights. Additionally, ethical concerns, particularly regarding privacy and decision-making biases, need to be carefully managed to avoid the misuse of predictive analytics.

Integration with Business Strategies

To fully leverage predictive analytics, businesses need to integrate these insights into their strategic planning and operational processes. This integration requires not only the right tools and technologies but also a change in mindset at all levels of the organization. Leaders must champion data-driven decision-making and encourage a culture of innovation and continuous improvement. Predictive analytics should also be combined with other forms of analytics to provide a holistic view. While predictive analytics can forecast future events, combining these forecasts with descriptive and prescriptive analytics provides a more comprehensive approach to data-driven decision-making.

Predictive analytics opens up a world of possibilities by allowing businesses to look into the future and make informed decisions that can provide them with a competitive edge. By understanding its methodologies, applying them across various sectors, and integrating them into business operations, organizations can not only foresee but also effectively shape their future. As we progress further into the age of data, the role of predictive analytics in everyday business processes will only become more entrenched, turning data into one of the most valuable assets a company can possess. In the next chapters, we will explore how these predictions can be translated into actionable strategies through prescriptive analytics, completing the analytics continuum from what has happened to what should happen next.

CHAPTER 7
Harnessing Prescriptive Analytics

Prescriptive analytics extends beyond the insights offered by predictive analytics by not only forecasting future outcomes but also recommending specific actions to achieve these desired outcomes. This chapter explores the methodologies, tools, and practical applications of prescriptive analytics, emphasizing how it transforms data insights into actionable strategies that drive business success. We delve into the advanced algorithms and decision-making frameworks that characterize prescriptive analytics, such as optimization models and simulation techniques. These tools help businesses navigate complex scenarios by suggesting the best courses of action based on predictive models and real-time data. The practical applications of prescriptive analytics are vast, ranging from supply chain optimization and resource allocation to customer experience enhancement and strategic planning. Through real-world case studies, this chapter illustrates how various industries leverage prescriptive analytics to not only predict future trends but also to proactively shape their outcomes, thereby securing a competitive edge and achieving operational excellence.

Defining Prescriptive Analytics

While predictive analytics focuses on forecasting future events, prescriptive analytics provides actionable recommendations on what actions to take. It answers the question, "What should we do?" by leveraging advanced algorithms, optimization models, and simulation techniques to suggest the best course of action. This capability is crucial for decision-makers who need to make informed choices that optimize outcomes and achieve strategic objectives.

At its core, prescriptive analytics integrates various forms of data analysis, including machine learning, statistical modeling, and operations research, to recommend decisions that maximize benefits and minimize risks. This approach is essential for addressing complex decision-making scenarios where multiple variables and potential outcomes must be considered simultaneously.

Key Techniques and Tools

Several techniques are central to prescriptive analytics:

- **Optimization Models**: These mathematical models are designed to find the best solution to a problem, considering constraints and objectives. Techniques such as linear programming, integer programming, and nonlinear optimization are widely used in fields like logistics, finance, and operations management. Optimization models help businesses allocate resources efficiently, schedule tasks effectively, and maximize profits while adhering to constraints.

- **Simulation and Modeling**: Simulation techniques model complex systems and processes to evaluate the impact of different decisions. Monte Carlo simulations, system dynamics, and agent-based modeling are commonly used to simulate various scenarios and predict outcomes. These tools allow businesses to test hypotheses, explore potential risks, and understand the implications of different strategies without real-world experimentation.

- **Machine Learning and AI**: Machine learning algorithms, including decision trees, neural networks, and reinforcement learning, are employed to develop models that recommend actions based on data patterns. These algorithms can learn from historical data, adapt to new information, and improve their recommendations over time, making them invaluable for dynamic decision environments.

Applications across Industries

Prescriptive analytics has diverse applications across various sectors:

- **Supply Chain Optimization**: In supply chain management, prescriptive analytics helps optimize inventory levels, streamline logistics, and enhance demand forecasting. By analyzing historical data and real-time information, businesses can make informed decisions on inventory replenishment, reduce stockouts, and minimize excess inventory, thereby improving operational efficiency and customer satisfaction.

- **Financial Planning and Risk Management**: Financial institutions use prescriptive analytics for portfolio optimization, risk assessment, and fraud detection. Algorithms recommend investment strategies, evaluate credit risk, and identify suspicious transactions, enabling banks and investment firms to manage risks effectively and enhance returns.

- **Healthcare Management**: In healthcare, prescriptive analytics is used to develop personalized treatment plans, optimize resource allocation, and improve patient outcomes. By analyzing patient data, medical history, and treatment responses, healthcare providers can recommend the most effective treatments, allocate resources efficiently, and reduce healthcare costs.

- **Marketing and Customer Engagement**: Marketers leverage prescriptive analytics to design targeted marketing campaigns, optimize pricing strategies, and enhance customer segmentation. By analyzing customer data and predicting behavior, businesses can personalize marketing efforts, increase customer engagement, and boost sales.

Implementing Prescriptive Analytics

Integrating prescriptive analytics into business processes requires a strategic approach:

- **Data Integration and Quality**: Successful prescriptive analytics relies on high-quality, integrated data from various sources. Organizations must invest in data infrastructure, ensuring data consistency, accuracy, and accessibility. Data lakes, cloud storage, and data warehouses play a crucial role in consolidating and managing large volumes of data.

- **Technology and Tools**: Businesses must choose the right tools and platforms to support prescriptive analytics. Popular tools include IBM Watson, SAP Predictive Analytics, and Microsoft Azure Machine Learning, which offer comprehensive solutions for data analysis, modeling, and decision support. These tools provide the computational power and analytics capabilities needed to develop and deploy prescriptive models effectively.

- **Skill Development and Change Management**: Building a culture that embraces data-driven decision-making is essential. Organizations should invest in training and development programs to enhance the analytical skills of their workforce. Additionally, change management strategies are crucial for fostering acceptance and adoption of prescriptive analytics across the organization.

Challenges and Considerations

Despite its benefits, prescriptive analytics presents several challenges:

- **Complexity and Cost**: Developing and implementing prescriptive analytics solutions can be complex and costly. Organizations need to invest in advanced technologies, skilled personnel, and ongoing maintenance to ensure the effectiveness of their analytics initiatives.

- **Ethical and Privacy Concerns**: As prescriptive analytics often involves sensitive data, ethical considerations and privacy concerns are paramount. Businesses must ensure compliance with data protection regulations and implement robust security measures to safeguard customer data and maintain trust.

- **Integration with Existing Systems**: Integrating prescriptive analytics into existing IT systems and workflows can be challenging. Organizations must ensure seamless interoperability between new analytics tools and legacy systems, facilitating smooth data flow and decision-making processes.

Prescriptive analytics empowers organizations to move from data-driven insights to actionable strategies, enhancing decision-making and driving business performance. By leveraging advanced algorithms and simulation techniques, businesses can optimize their operations, mitigate risks, and seize opportunities with confidence.

As we continue to explore the potential of analytics, the next chapter will focus on real-world case studies, showcasing how companies have successfully implemented prescriptive analytics to achieve remarkable outcomes. These examples will illustrate the transformative impact of prescriptive analytics across various industries, providing practical insights and inspiration for your own analytics journey.

CHAPTER 8
Real-World Applications of Analytics across Industries

Analytics has revolutionized multiple industries by offering more profound insights into operational efficiencies, customer behaviors, and evolving market trends. This chapter delves into detailed case studies from a diverse array of sectors, showcasing how companies harness the power of descriptive, predictive, and prescriptive analytics to enhance their decision-making processes and achieve significant results. These analytics types help businesses understand past and current data (descriptive), forecast future scenarios (predictive), and suggest actionable strategies (prescriptive). By examining real-world applications in sectors such as healthcare, retail, finance, and manufacturing, the text demonstrates how data-driven strategies are effectively integrated into business models.

For instance, in healthcare, analytics predict patient outcomes and optimize treatment plans, while in retail, it aids in managing stock levels and personalizing customer experiences. Financial services use these tools for risk assessment and fraud detection, and manufacturing sectors improve supply chain efficiency and product quality. Through these case studies, the chapter illustrates the transformative impact of analytics, providing businesses with the tools they need to not only interpret complex datasets but also to enact operational changes that drive substantial growth and efficiency.

Case Studies across Diverse Sectors

Retail Sector: Optimizing Inventory and Enhancing Customer Experience

A major retail chain implemented predictive analytics to enhance its inventory management and improve customer satisfaction. By analyzing sales data, customer feedback, and supply chain logistics, the company developed models that predicted future product demands with high accuracy. This allowed them to adjust inventory in real-time, reducing overstock and understock situations, which significantly cut down on storage and capital costs. Moreover, prescriptive analytics was used to tailor marketing campaigns to individual consumer preferences, which boosted customer engagement and increased sales. This holistic approach to data-driven decision-making exemplifies how analytics can transform traditional retail operations into dynamic and responsive systems.

Healthcare: Improving Patient Outcomes and Operational Efficiency

In the healthcare industry, a renowned hospital used prescriptive analytics to optimize its patient flow and resource allocation. By integrating patient data—from admission to discharge—into a centralized analytics system, the hospital could forecast patient influx during different times of the year and adjust staffing levels accordingly. Predictive analytics also identified patients at high risk of readmission, allowing healthcare providers to intervene earlier with preventive measures. This not only improved patient outcomes but also reduced the burden on hospital resources and decreased operational costs.

Manufacturing: Enhancing Productivity and Predictive Maintenance

A leading manufacturer of automotive parts utilized predictive analytics to foresee equipment failures before they occurred. By collecting and analyzing data from machine sensors, the company developed predictive models that alerted maintenance teams about potential issues. This proactive approach to maintenance—often referred to as predictive maintenance—helped the company avoid unplanned downtime, which is costly and disruptive. Furthermore, prescriptive analytics provided recommendations for optimizing production schedules and workflows, leading to increased productivity and reduced operational costs.

Financial Services: Fraud Detection and Risk Management

A global bank implemented advanced analytics to enhance its fraud detection capabilities and manage credit risks more effectively. Using machine learning algorithms, the bank analyzed transaction patterns and customer profiles to detect anomalous behavior indicative of fraud. This predictive capability allowed them to prevent substantial financial losses and protect customer accounts. Additionally, prescriptive analytics offered insights into customers' creditworthiness, enabling more accurate risk assessment and tailored loan offerings. This not only minimized defaults but also improved customer satisfaction by providing them with personalized financial solutions.

Transportation: Streamlining Operations and Improving Service Delivery

A transportation and logistics company integrated descriptive and predictive analytics to overhaul its route planning and fleet management operations. By analyzing historical traffic data, weather reports, and vehicle performance metrics, predictive models were developed to suggest optimal routes and schedules. This reduced fuel consumption and improved delivery times, significantly enhancing customer satisfaction. Prescriptive analytics further aided in strategic decision-making, recommending fleet expansions and contractions based on forecasted demand, thereby optimizing operational efficiency and cost-effectiveness.

Energy Sector: Optimizing Production and Sustainable Practices

An energy company utilized predictive and prescriptive analytics to enhance its production efficiency and embrace more sustainable practices. By analyzing data from various sensors across its operations, predictive models forecasted energy demand spikes and dips, allowing for better alignment of energy production with actual needs. This optimized energy use reduced waste and operational costs. Prescriptive models went further, suggesting adjustments in resource allocation and investment in renewable energy sources, supporting the company's goals for sustainability and compliance with environmental regulations.

Challenges and Lessons Learned

These case studies not only showcase the transformative power of analytics across various industries but also underscore the prevalent challenges encountered during their implementation. Deploying analytics solutions demands meticulous planning, significant investments in technology and talent, and a steadfast commitment to cultivating a data-driven culture within the organization. Common hurdles include issues like data silos, which hinder effective data integration, quality concerns that can compromise analytics outcomes, and organizational resistance to change, which can stifle innovation. The lessons drawn from these experiences highlight the critical importance of obtaining executive support, fostering collaboration through cross-functional teams, and promoting an environment of continuous learning and adaptation. These elements are essential to overcoming challenges and maximizing the benefits of analytics initiatives, thereby enabling organizations to leverage data insights more effectively and drive substantial improvements.

The real-world applications of analytics presented in this chapter demonstrate that when effectively implemented, analytics can profoundly impact business operations, strategic decision-making, and customer interactions. These case studies across various sectors showcase the practical benefits of integrating descriptive, predictive, and prescriptive analytics into business processes. As companies continue to navigate the complexities of the modern business environment, analytics will remain a crucial tool for driving innovation, efficiency, and competitive advantage.

The insights gained from these applications not only inspire but also provide a roadmap for other organizations aiming to leverage analytics to solve complex business challenges. Moving forward, the adoption of advanced analytics is expected to grow, with more businesses realizing its potential to transform their operations and achieve significant returns on investment.

CHAPTER 9

Navigating Challenges and Ethical Considerations in Data Analytics

The journey through data analytics, while rewarding, is fraught with challenges and ethical dilemmas. This chapter provides a thorough exploration of the common obstacles that businesses encounter when implementing analytics solutions. It also delves into the crucial ethical considerations that must be addressed to preserve trust and integrity within data-driven decision-making processes. Businesses often face technical hurdles, such as integrating complex data systems and ensuring data accuracy and security. Additionally, there are human factors, including skill shortages and resistance to change among staff. On the ethical front, concerns about privacy, consent, and the potential for bias in data models are paramount. Addressing these issues requires transparent data practices, continuous ethical training for analytics personnel, and stringent data governance policies. This chapter aims to equip readers with the knowledge to navigate these challenges effectively, emphasizing the importance of ethical standards to maintain credibility and trust in analytics initiatives.

Overcoming Challenges in Data Analytics

As organizations strive to harness the power of data analytics, they encounter a variety of challenges that can impede their progress. These challenges range from technical issues to organizational and cultural barriers.

Technical Challenges: One of the primary technical challenges is managing large volumes of data, often referred to as "Big Data." The storage, processing, and analysis of this data require robust IT infrastructure and powerful analytical tools. Data quality and integration also pose significant challenges, as data collected from various sources can be inconsistent, incomplete, or inaccurate. Developing effective methods for data cleaning and integration is crucial for ensuring that analytics outputs are reliable and actionable.

Organizational Challenges: Beyond the technical aspects, organizational challenges often arise, particularly in the form of resistance to change. Traditional businesses may struggle to shift from intuition-based to data-driven decision-making. This cultural shift requires not only educating and training employees on the value of analytics but also demonstrating how data-driven decisions can lead to better outcomes. Additionally, the siloed nature of some organizations can prevent the free flow of information, hindering the effectiveness of analytics initiatives.

Scalability Challenges: As analytics initiatives expand, scaling them to keep pace with growing business needs can be difficult. Scalability issues often involve integrating advanced analytics capabilities across various business units and ensuring that the infrastructure can handle increased loads. Addressing these challenges requires a scalable architecture and ongoing investments in technology and personnel.

Ethical Considerations in Data Analytics

Ethical considerations are increasingly coming to the forefront as analytics becomes more pervasive in decision-making processes. The primary ethical concerns revolve around privacy, consent, bias, and transparency.

Privacy and Consent: With the vast amounts of data being collected, ensuring the privacy of individuals is paramount. Organizations must handle data responsibly, complying with regulations such as the General Data Protection Regulation (GDPR) in Europe and other local data protection laws. This involves obtaining consent from individuals before collecting their data and ensuring that the data is used solely for the purposes specified.

Bias and Fairness: Algorithms used in data analytics can sometimes perpetuate or even exacerbate biases present in the data. This can lead to unfair outcomes, particularly in sensitive areas such as hiring, lending, and law enforcement. Organizations must be vigilant in identifying and mitigating biases in their data sets and algorithms. This can involve employing techniques such as fairness-aware modeling and conducting regular audits of algorithmic processes.

Transparency and Accountability: Maintaining transparency in how data is collected, analyzed, and used is essential for building trust with stakeholders. This means being open about the methodologies used in analytics processes and the decisions driven by analytics. Moreover, accountability mechanisms should be in place to address any issues or harms that arise from analytics-driven decisions.

Case Studies in Ethical Data Use

Healthcare: A hospital implemented a predictive analytics system to identify patients at risk of chronic diseases. However, they faced ethical questions about patient privacy and the potential for bias in the algorithm, which was initially trained on a dataset that was not representative of the diverse patient population it served. The hospital addressed these issues by revising its data collection and model training processes and implementing stringent data security measures.

Finance: A financial institution uses prescriptive analytics to optimize its loan offerings. The challenge was to ensure that the algorithms did not discriminate against any group, inadvertently denying loans based on biased data. To combat this, the institution employed fairness-aware algorithms and regularly reviewed its decision-making processes to ensure compliance with ethical lending practices.

Retail: A retail company used customer data to personalize marketing strategies. The ethical challenge was to balance effective marketing with respect for customer privacy. The company ensured that all marketing strategies were compliant with data protection laws and that customers had clear options to opt out of data collection and personalization.

Navigating the challenges and ethical considerations of data analytics requires a multifaceted approach involving technological solutions, organizational strategies, and a strong ethical framework. By addressing these challenges head-on and committing to ethical practices, organizations can not only enhance their analytics capabilities but also maintain the trust and loyalty of their customers and stakeholders.

In the final chapter, we will explore the future of data analytics, focusing on emerging trends and technologies that are set to redefine how businesses leverage data for competitive advantage. This forward-looking perspective will provide readers with insights into staying ahead in the rapidly evolving field of data analytics.

CHAPTER 10
The Future of Data Analytics: Trends and Innovations

As we conclude our exploration of data analytics, it is crucial to look ahead and consider the emerging trends and technologies that are set to reshape the landscape of business intelligence. This chapter delves into the future of data analytics, emphasizing how advancements in technology and evolving business practices are poised to influence data-driven decision-making. We will explore cutting-edge developments such as artificial intelligence (AI) and machine learning algorithms that are becoming increasingly sophisticated, offering businesses unprecedented insights and predictive capabilities. Additionally, the rise of big data and the expansion of Internet of Things (IoT) devices are generating vast amounts of data, providing more opportunities for deep analytics. We also consider shifts in business practices, such as the increasing demand for real-time data processing and the growing importance of data ethics and privacy. This chapter aims to provide a comprehensive overview of the trends that will define the next generation of analytics, preparing businesses to not only adapt to these changes but also to thrive in an increasingly data-centric world.

Advancements in Artificial Intelligence and Machine Learning

The integration of artificial intelligence (AI) and machine learning (ML) with data analytics is rapidly advancing, offering unprecedented capabilities for automated decision-making and predictive analytics. AI technologies, especially deep learning, are becoming more sophisticated, allowing for more accurate predictions and smarter prescriptive analytics. These technologies can process and analyze vast amounts of data in real-time, enabling businesses to respond more swiftly to market changes and consumer behaviors.

One of the key areas where AI is making a significant impact is in natural language processing (NLP). NLP technologies are improving at understanding and generating human language, which opens up new avenues for automated customer service and insights from unstructured data like social media posts, customer reviews, and open-ended survey responses. As AI continues to evolve, we can expect more intuitive interfaces and systems that can "think" more like humans, making data analytics more accessible to all levels of an organization.

The Rise of Edge Computing

Edge computing is set to play a crucial role in the future of data analytics by processing data at the edge of the network, closer to where it is generated. This is particularly important for the Internet of Things (IoT) and mobile applications, where sending vast amounts of data to a central server for processing can cause delays and increase costs. By processing data locally, businesses can achieve faster response times and reduce bandwidth usage, which is essential for applications that require real-time analysis, such as autonomous vehicles, manufacturing processes, and smart cities.

Increased Emphasis on Data Governance and Security

As data breaches continue to pose significant risks, the importance of data governance and security in analytics is more pronounced than ever. Businesses will need to invest heavily in secure data storage solutions, robust data governance policies, and advanced security protocols to protect sensitive information. This includes the implementation of more sophisticated encryption technologies, regular security audits, and compliance with international data protection regulations. Furthermore, there will be an increased focus on ethical data usage, ensuring that data is not only secure but also used responsibly and transparently.

Democratization of Data Analytics

The democratization of data analytics refers to making analytics tools more accessible to non-experts, allowing more people within an organization to make informed decisions without the need for specialized training. This trend is supported by the development of user-friendly analytics platforms that integrate AI assistants and automated insights, making complex data analysis more accessible to everyone. As these tools become more prevalent, we can expect a shift in how decisions are made, with a more collaborative and informed approach across all levels of an organization.

Personalization and Predictive Customer Insights

In marketing and customer relationship management, the future of data analytics lies in personalization and predictive insights. Businesses are increasingly using data analytics to predict customer behaviors, personalize marketing messages, and optimize customer experiences. This trend is about understanding the individual preferences and behaviors of customers to tailor products, services, and interactions to meet their specific needs. As analytics tools become more advanced, the ability to predict customer needs and respond proactively will be a key differentiator for businesses.

Sustainable Analytics

As global awareness of environmental issues grows, businesses are also looking at how data analytics can contribute to sustainability. This includes using analytics to optimize energy use, reduce waste, and streamline operations to minimize environmental impact. Sustainable analytics also involves using data to monitor and improve the environmental footprint of business activities, helping companies to meet regulatory requirements and consumer expectations for corporate responsibility.

The future of data analytics is characterized by rapid advancements in technology, a greater focus on security and ethical considerations, and the increasing importance of real-time and predictive insights. As businesses continue to navigate a data-driven world, staying abreast of these trends and innovations will be crucial for maintaining competitive advantage and achieving sustainable growth.

By embracing these future directions, organizations can ensure that they are not only prepared to handle the challenges of tomorrow but are also positioned to lead with innovation and strategic insight. This proactive approach to future trends in data analytics will empower businesses to continue transforming data into actionable intelligence that drives decision-making and fosters long-term success.

FAQs

Here are some frequently asked questions (FAQs) related to data analytics, designed to help clarify common queries and deepen understanding of the field:

1. What is data analytics? Data analytics involves examining raw data with the purpose of drawing conclusions and identifying patterns. It encompasses a variety of techniques and processes automated into mechanical processes and algorithms that work over raw data for human consumption.

2. How does predictive analytics differ from prescriptive analytics? Predictive analytics uses historical data to predict future outcomes, employing statistical models and machine learning techniques. Prescriptive analytics goes a step further by not only predicting what will happen but also suggesting actions and outlining potential effects of each decision path.

3. What are the key skills needed to become a data analyst? Key skills include statistical analysis, data visualization, knowledge of programming languages like Python or R, proficiency with analytics software (such as SAS or Tableau), and strong problem-solving abilities.

4. What is Big Data? Big Data refers to extremely large data sets that may be analyzed computationally to reveal patterns, trends, and associations, especially relating to human behavior and interactions.

5. How can small businesses benefit from data analytics? Small businesses can use data analytics to gain insights into customer behavior, improve operational efficiency, optimize marketing campaigns, and enhance decision-making, leading to increased profitability and competitive advantage.

6. What are some common tools used in data analytics? Common tools include SQL for database management, Python and R for statistical analysis, and specialized software like Tableau for data visualization, as well as Excel for simpler analytics tasks.

7. What are the ethical considerations in data analytics? Ethical considerations include ensuring privacy and security of data, obtaining data through fair and legal means, avoiding biased data which can lead to skewed outcomes, and maintaining transparency about data use with stakeholders.

8. How is AI used in data analytics? AI is used to automate complex analytical tasks, enhance the accuracy of models through deep learning, improve the efficiency of data processing, and enable more sophisticated prediction and optimization capabilities.

9. What industries benefit the most from data analytics? While almost all industries can benefit from data analytics, sectors such as finance, healthcare, marketing, retail, and manufacturing see significant improvements in decision-making, customer satisfaction, efficiency, and profitability through data analytics.

10. How can I ensure the security of my data analytics processes? To secure data analytics processes, implement robust data encryption, use secure data storage solutions, conduct regular security audits, adhere to compliance standards like GDPR, and continually update security protocols to address new vulnerabilities.